This Book Belongs To:

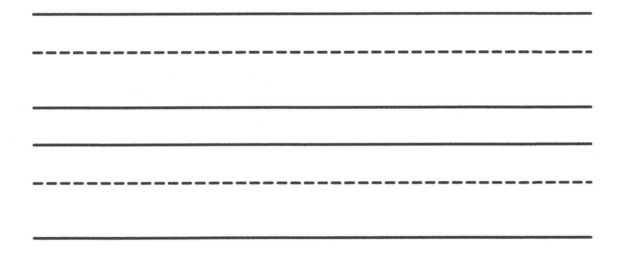

D1451520

Write the missing number

□ 1 2 3 4 5 6 7 8 9 10

0   zero

Trace and Write the Number 0

0 0 0 0 0 0

0

zero zero

Write the missing number

0 ☐ 2 3 4 5 6 7 8 9 10

1

one

Trace and Write the Number 1

one one one

Write the missing number

0 1 ☐ 3 4 5 6 7 8 9 10

2 † two

Trace and Write the Number 2

2 2 2 2 2 2 2

2

two two two

Write the missing number

0 1 2 ☐ 4 5 6 7 8 9 10

3   three

Trace and Write the Number 3

3 3 3 3 3 3 3

3

three three

Write the missing number

0 1 2 3 ☐ 5 6 7 8 9 10

4   four

Trace and Write the Number 4

four   four

Write the missing number

0 1 2 3 4 ☐ 6 7 8 9 10

5   five

Trace and Write the Number 5

5 5 5 5 5 5 5 5 5

5

five five five

Write the missing number

0 1 2 3 4 5 ☐ 7 8 9 10

6   six

Trace and Write the Number 6

6 6 6 6 6 6 6

6

six   six   six

Write the missing number

0 1 2 3 4 5 6 ☐ 8 9 10

7   seven

Trace and Write the Number 7

7 7 7 7 7 7 7 7

7

seven   seven

Write the missing number

0 1 2 3 4 5 6 7 □ 9 10

8   eight

Trace and Write the Number 8

8 8 8 8 8 8 8

8

eight   eight

Write the missing number

0 1 2 3 4 5 6 7 8 ☐ 10

9   nine

Trace and Write the Number 9

9 9 9 9 9 9 9 9 9

9

nine nine nine

Write the missing number

0 1 2 3 4 5 6 7 8 9 ☐

10 ten

Trace and Write the Number 10

10 10 10 10 10

10

ten ten ten

Match the numbers

Draw a line to match the number to its name.

3 •	• four
1 •	• seven
2 •	• five
6 •	• two
10 •	• ten
5 •	• nine
8 •	• one
4 •	• three
9 •	• six
7 •	• eight

How Many

Count the objects and write the correct
number in each box.

Skip Counting

Skip count and write the missing numbers to help the pirates find the treasure.

Before and After

Write the numbers that come before and after.

| 4 | 5 | 6 |

2

6

9

7

Before and After

Write the numbers that come before and after.

_____ 4 _____

_____ 8 _____

_____ 3 _____

_____ 1 _____

_____ 2 _____

How Many

Count the objects and write the number symbols in each box.

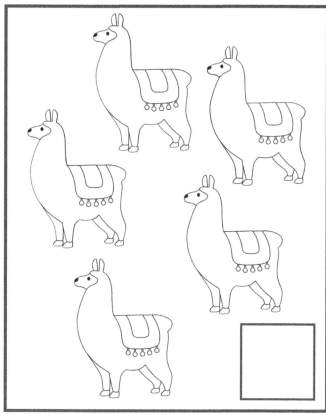

Count & Mark

Count the objects in each box and mark the correct number.

5   6   7   8

3   8   6   5

2   8   9   4

5   1   6   3

Before

Write the number that comes before these numbers.

3   4   5

     7   8

     3   4

     5   6

     8   9

Before

Write the number that comes before these numbers.

_____ 6 7

_____ 1 2

_____ 10 11

_____ 9 10

_____ 2 3

Skip Counting

Skip count and write the missing numbers.

1			4
5		7	
	10		12
		15	
17			20

Count & Mark

Count the objects in each box and mark the
correct number.

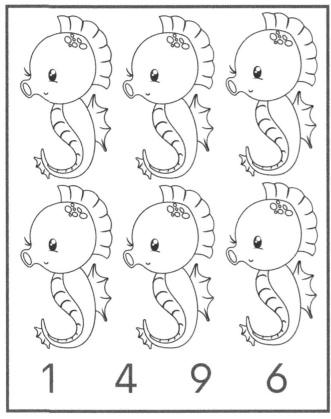

1   4   9   6

7   3   2   1

2   4   7   5

2   1   4   3

After

Write the number that comes after these numbers.

7   8   9

5   6

1   2

8   9

2   3

After

Write the number that comes after these numbers.

9   10

3   4

6   7

0   1

4   5

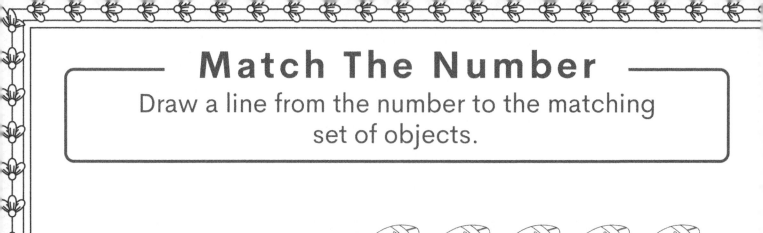

Match The Number

Draw a line from the number to the matching
set of objects.

3.

1.

9.

6.

How Many

Count the objects and write the correct
number in each box.

Between

Write the number that comes between these numbers.

2   3   4

5   7

9   11

0   2

6   8

Between

Write the number that comes between these numbers.

3 _____ 5

7 _____ 9

1 _____ 3

4 _____ 6

8 _____ 10

How Many

Count the objects and write the number symbols in each box.

Skip Counting

Skip count and write the missing numbers to help the bee find the right way to the flowers.

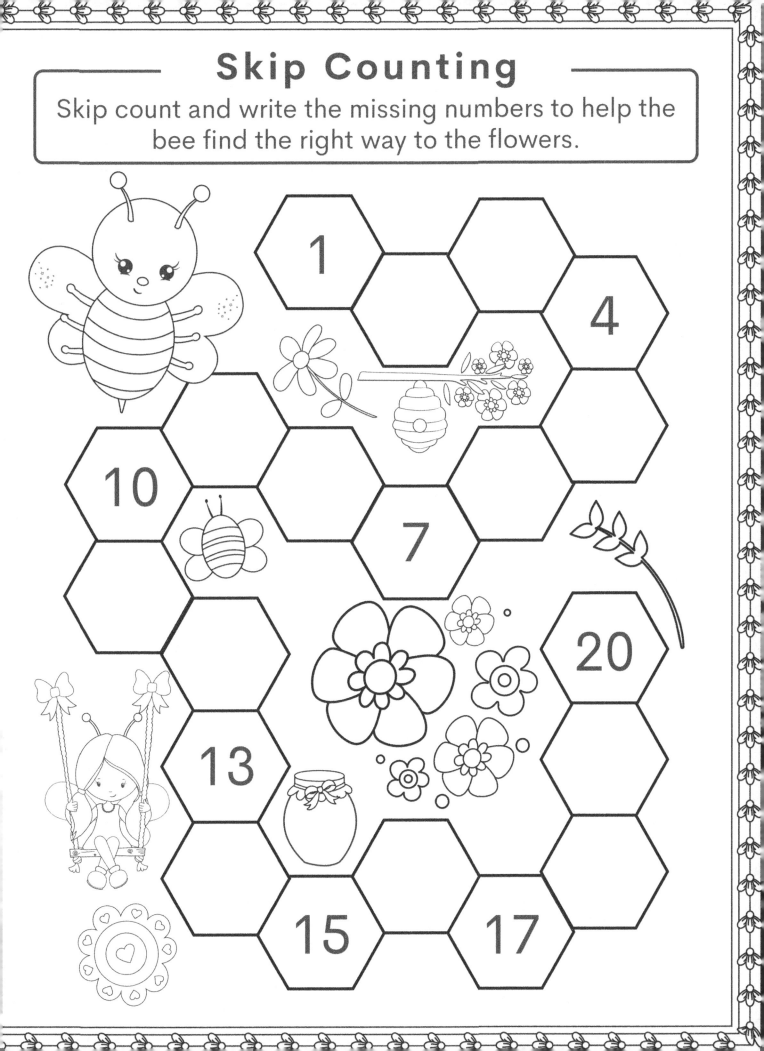

Before, Between, And After!

Write the numbers that come before, between, and after.

before	between	after
—— 5	4 —— 6	4 ——
—— 1	1 —— 3	8 ——
—— 7	8 ——10	2 ——
—— 3	5 —— 7	6 ——
—— 9	0 —— 2	5 ——

Count & Mark

Count the objects in each box and mark the
correct number.

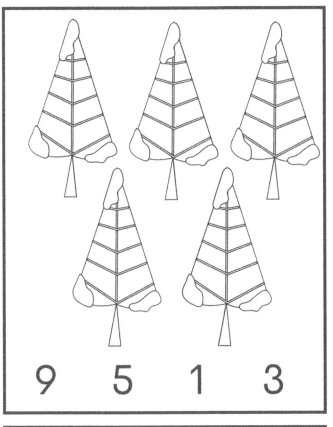

9   5   1   3

4   1   2   8

5   7   3   1

6   2   1   9

Greater Than, Less Than, Equal to

Write in each circle with the correct symbol.

> is greater than	= is equal to	< is less than
>	**=**	**<**
4 (>) 2	3 (=) 3	1 (<) 5
4 is greater than 2	3 is equal to 3	1 is less than 5

6 ◯ 4   2 ◯ 2

2 ◯ 7   3 ◯ 1

5 ◯ 5   4 ◯ 4

9 ◯ 8   10 ◯ 5

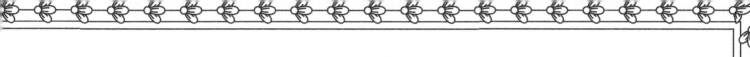

Greater Than, Less Than, Equal to

Write in each circle with the correct symbol.

8 ◯ 4   9 ◯ 9

1 ◯ 1   7 ◯ 5

7 ◯ 9   6 ◯ 4

4 ◯ 3   2 ◯ 7

1 ◯ 6   9 ◯ 3

2 ◯ 2   5 ◯ 8

Greater Than, Less Than, Equal to

Count the objects and write the correct symbol in each circle.

> is greater than   = is equal to   < is less than

Greater Than Or Less Than

Write the correct number of objects on the circle then choose greater or less to complete the sentences.

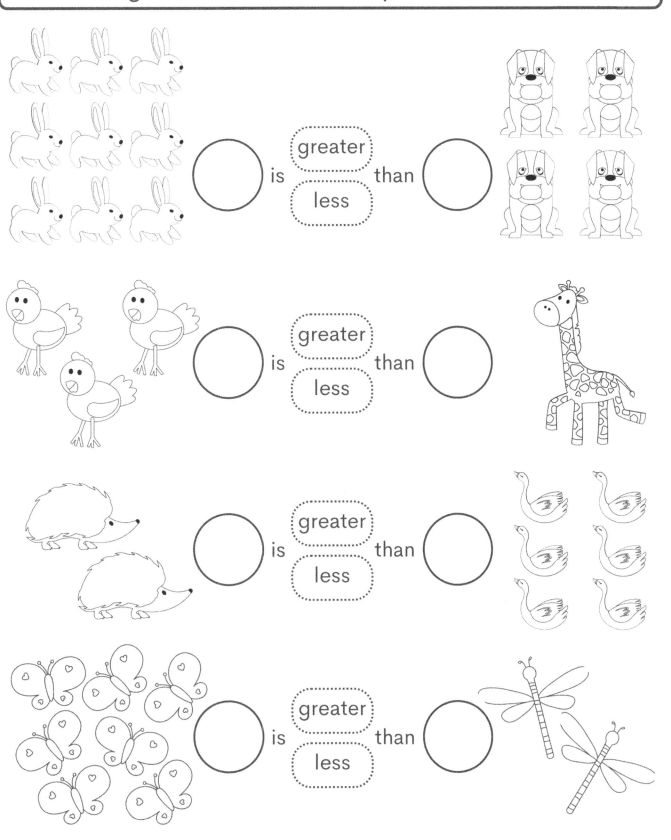

( ) is greater / less than ( )

( ) is greater / less than ( )

( ) is greater / less than ( )

( ) is greater / less than ( )

Greater Than, Less Than, Equal to

Count the objects and write the correct
symbol in each circle.

> is greater than   = is equal to   < is less than

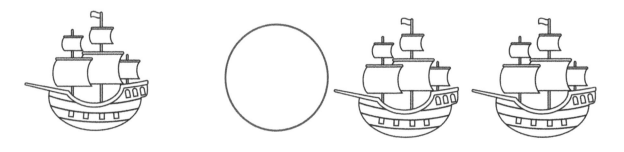

Greater Than Or Less Than

Write the correct number of objects on the circle then choose greater or less to complete the sentences.

Match The Number

Draw a line from the number to the matching
set of objects.

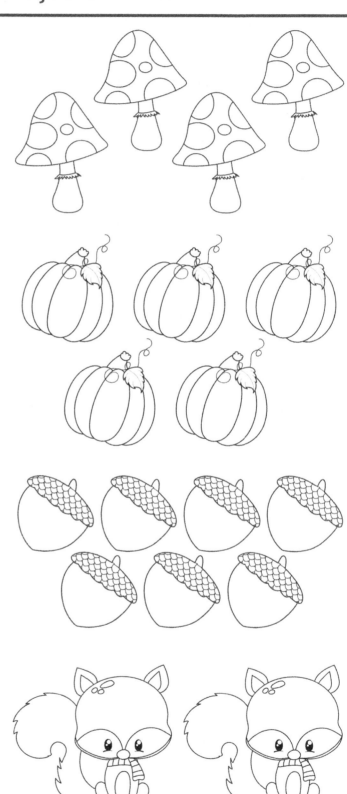

7.

4.

2.

5.

How Many

Count the objects and write the correct number in each box.

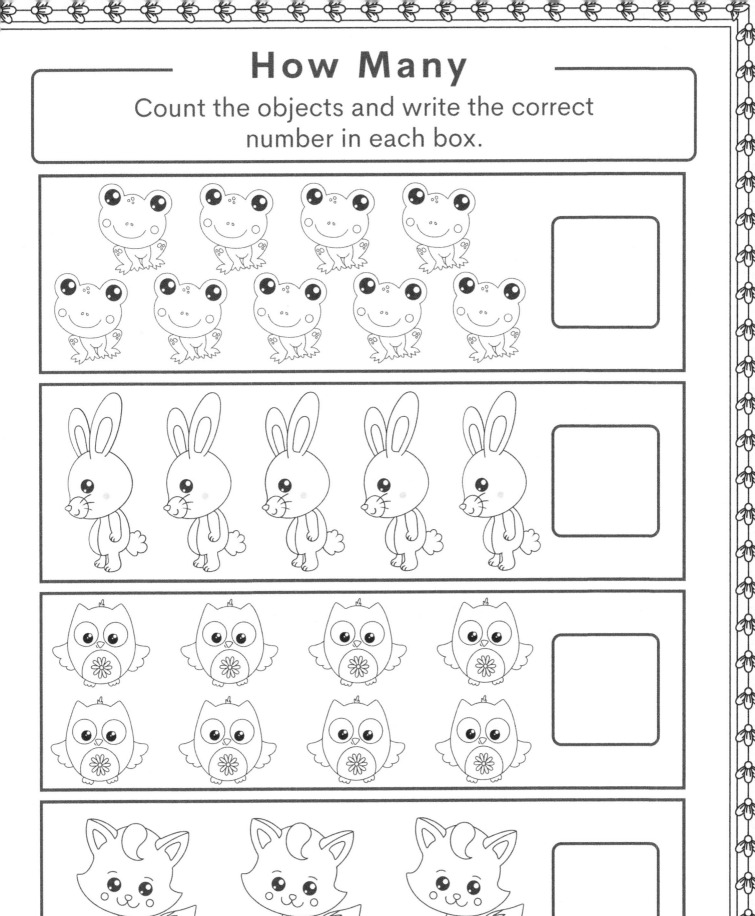

Skip Counting

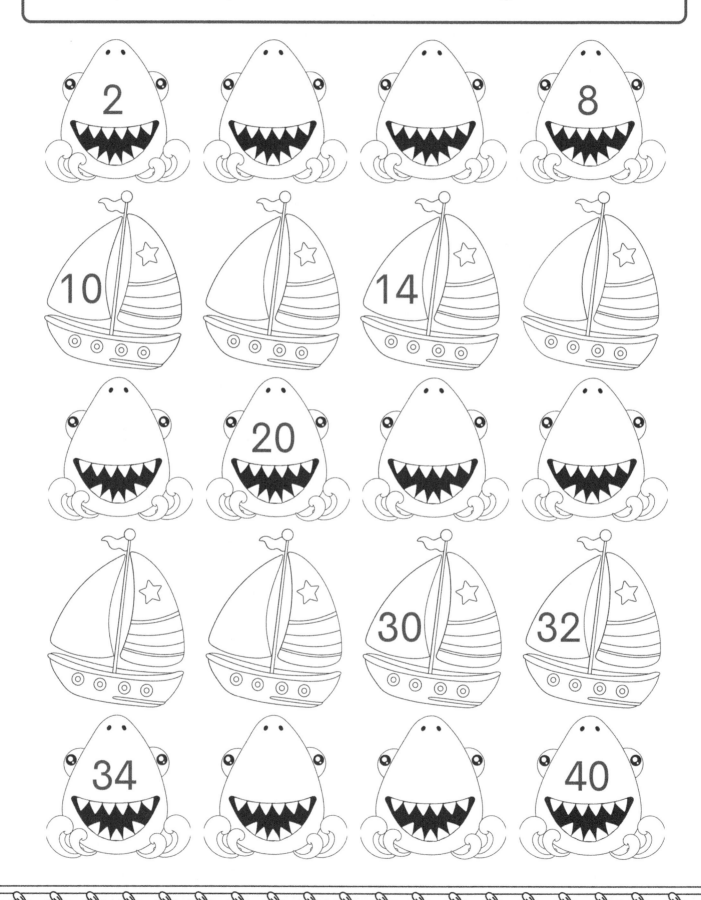

Count & Mark

Count the objects in each box and mark the correct number.

5   9   2   4

4   5   9   2

3   8   7   4

2   8   1   5

More or Less

Compare the two numbers in each row. Circle more or less to complete each sentence correctly.

2 is (more) (less) than 1

4 is (more) (less) than 5

9 is (more) (less) than 3

7 is (more) (less) than 8

Count And Match

Count the number of objects in each set and
draw a line to the matching number.

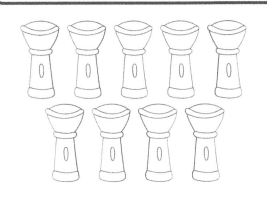

3

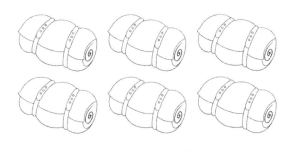

1

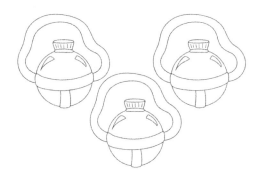

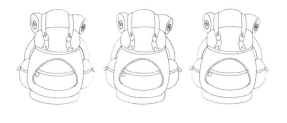

9

6

Skip Counting

Skip count by 2 and write the missing numbers.

Count And Match

Count the number of objects in each set and draw a line to the matching number.

5

4

2

7

More or Less

Compare the two numbers in each row. Circle more or less to complete each sentence correctly.

1 is (more) (less) than 6

2 is (more) (less) than 4

5 is (more) (less) than 3

7 is (more) (less) than 6

How Many

Count the objects and write the number symbols in each box.

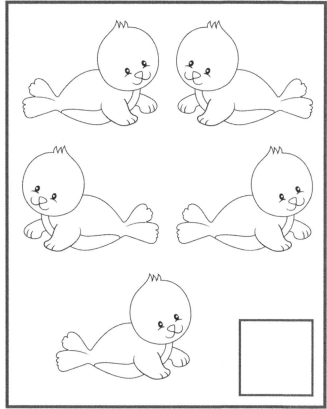

Skip Counting

Skip count by 2 and write the missing numbers to help the train reach the station.

Make 10

Find the missing numbers to make each part
of the wheel total 10.

Addition

Write the correct answer after the equal sign.

$$9 + 1 = \underline{\quad\quad}$$

$$3 + 4 = \underline{\quad\quad}$$

$$6 + 2 = \underline{\quad\quad}$$

$$4 + 5 = \underline{\quad\quad}$$

Addition

Add each set of objects and write the correct answer after the equal sign.

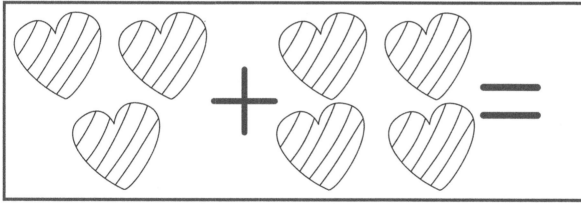

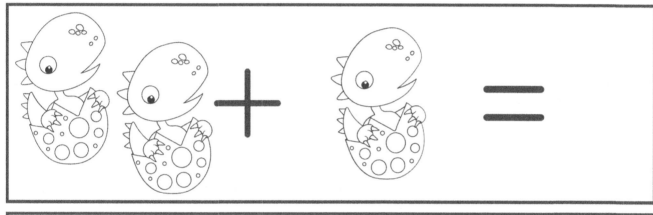

Subtraction

Find the missing number to solve each subtraction equation.

$$6 - \underline{\hspace{2cm}} = 2$$

$$10 - \underline{\hspace{2cm}} = 6$$

$$5 - \underline{\hspace{2cm}} = 4$$

$$3 - \underline{\hspace{2cm}} = 1$$

Subtraction

Write the correct answer after the equal sign.

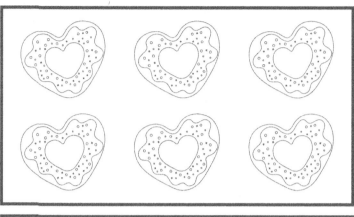 $6 - 4 =$ _____

 $9 - 2 =$ _____

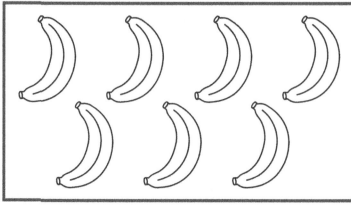 $5 - 1 =$ _____

 $7 - 5 =$ _____

Addition

Write the correct answer after the equal sign.

$5 + 3 =$ _____

$2 + 7 =$ _____

$7 + 0 =$ _____

$1 + 4 =$ _____

Addition

Miranda had 4 shells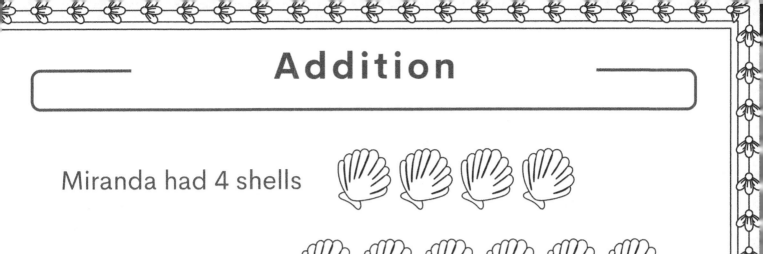

She found 6 more

How many shells does she have in all?

$$\boxed{} + \boxed{} = \boxed{}$$

Jack has 2 guitars at home

and 1 guitar at school

How many guitars does Jack have in all?

$$\boxed{} + \boxed{} = \boxed{}$$

Dice Addition

Add the numbers together to find the total.

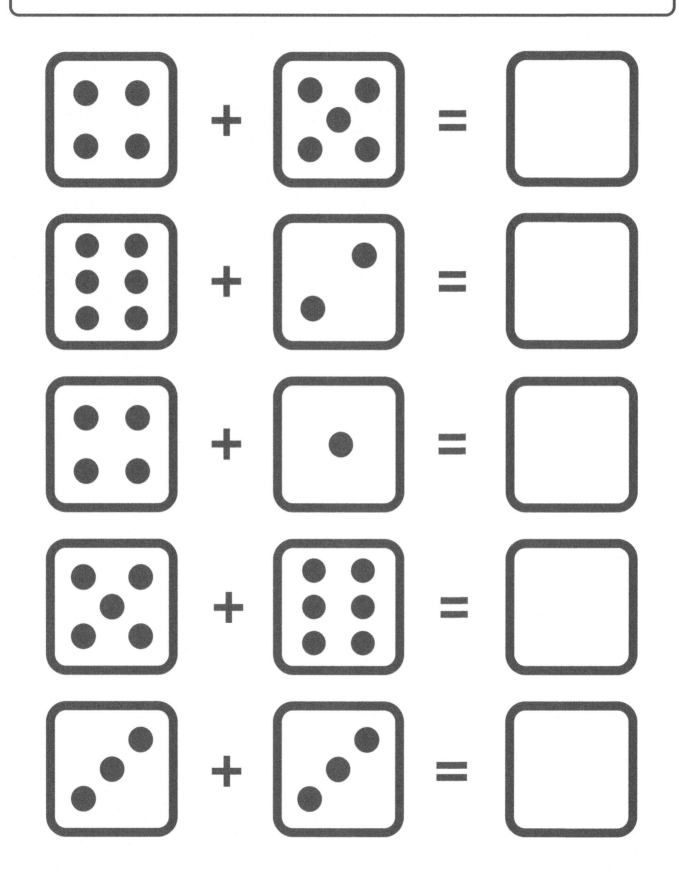

4 + 5 = ☐

6 + 2 = ☐

4 + 1 = ☐

5 + 6 = ☐

3 + 3 = ☐

Add And Match

Add the objects in each box and draw a line to match
with the correct number.

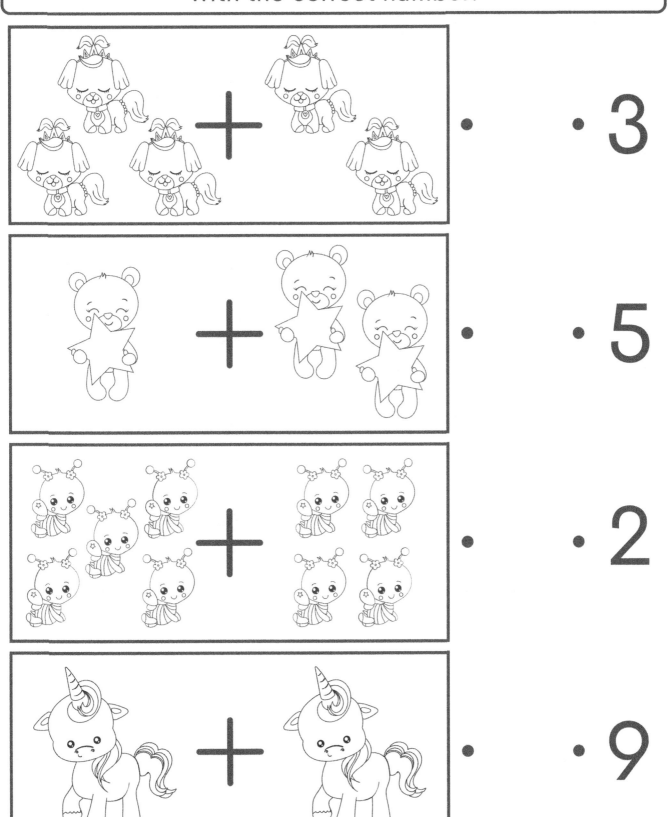

Subtraction

Write the correct answer after the equal sign.

$2 - 1 =$ _____

$7 - 3 =$ _____

$8 - 5 =$ _____

$9 - 0 =$ _____

Subtraction

Matthew had 3 notebooks at home

He took 1 notebook to school

How many notebooks did he leave at home?

$$\square - \square = \square$$

5 bees were sitting on a flower

3 bees flew away

How many bees are left?

$$\square - \square = \square$$

Addition

Find the missing number to solve each addition equation.

$$1 + \underline{\quad} = 3$$

$$4 + \underline{\quad} = 7$$

$$2 + \underline{\quad} = 5$$

$$6 + \underline{\quad} = 9$$

Addition

Add each set of objects and write the correct answer after the equal sign.

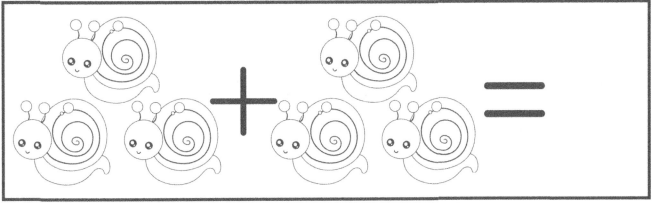

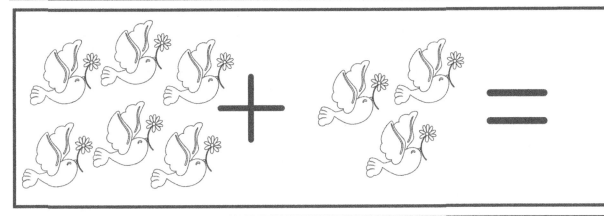

Subtraction

Write the correct answer after the equal sign.

$$8 - 2 = \underline{\hspace{3cm}}$$

$$4 - 1 = \underline{\hspace{3cm}}$$

$$3 - 3 = \underline{\hspace{3cm}}$$

$$6 - 4 = \underline{\hspace{3cm}}$$

Subtraction

Write the correct answer after the equal sign.

$$8 - 7 =$$

_____

$$6 - 3 =$$

_____

$$3 - 2 =$$

_____

$$5 - 1 =$$

_____

Addition

Find the missing number to solve each addition equation.

$$8 + \underline{\hspace{2cm}} = 9$$

$$9 + \underline{\hspace{2cm}} = 10$$

$$3 + \underline{\hspace{2cm}} = 6$$

$$5 + \underline{\hspace{2cm}} = 8$$

Addition

Melissa has a dog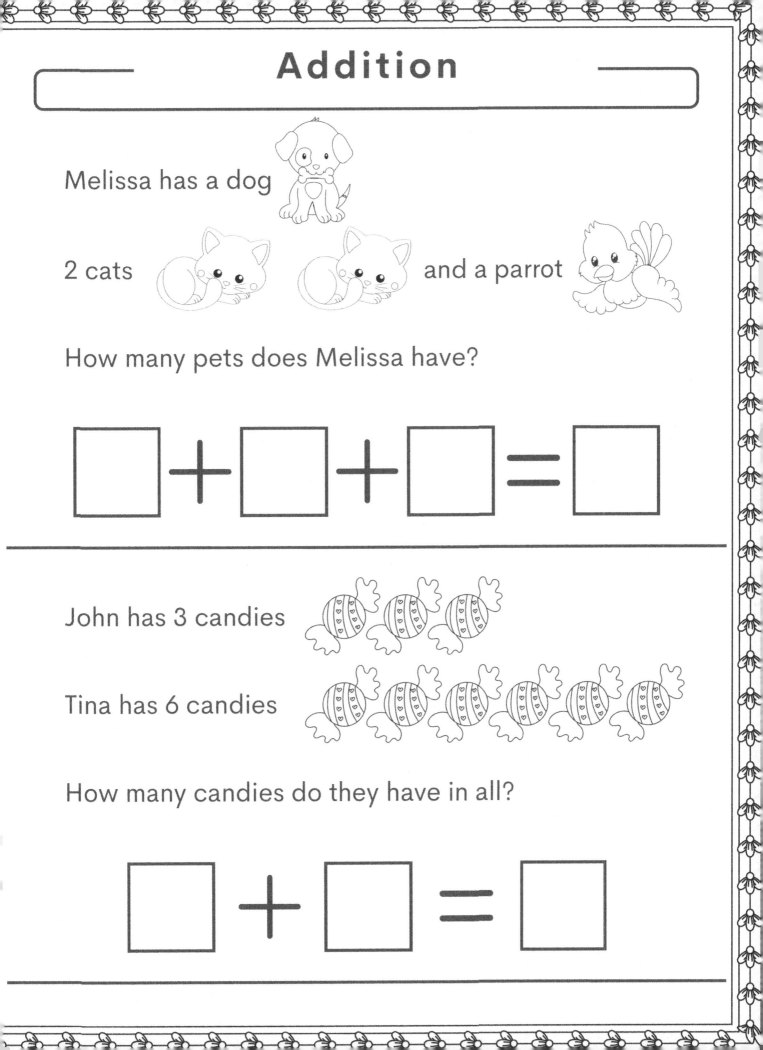

2 cats   and a parrot

How many pets does Melissa have?

$$\boxed{} + \boxed{} + \boxed{} = \boxed{}$$

John has 3 candies

Tina has 6 candies

How many candies do they have in all?

$$\boxed{} + \boxed{} = \boxed{}$$

Dice Addition

Add the numbers together to find the total.

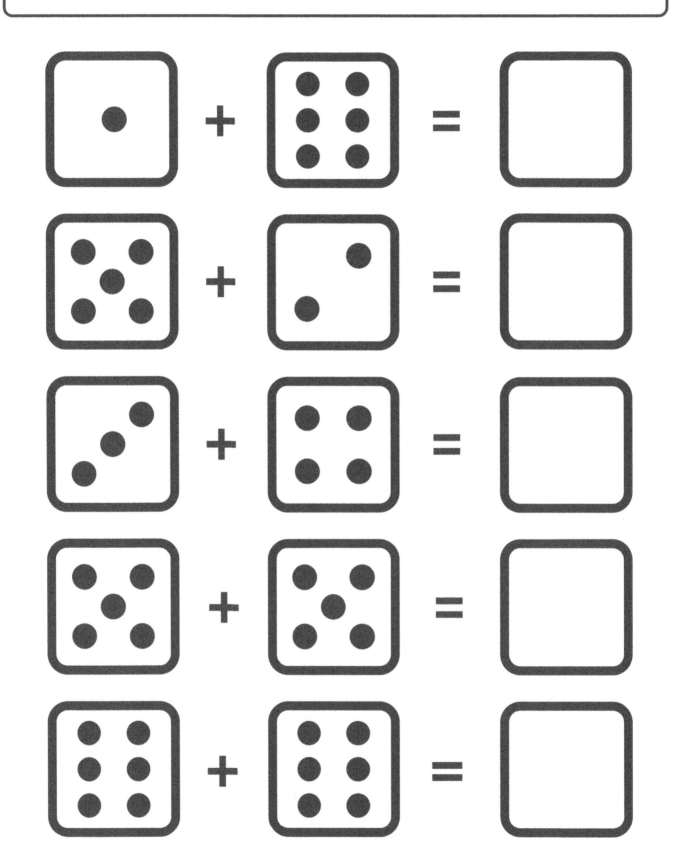

Add And Match

Add the objects in each box and draw a line to match with the correct number.

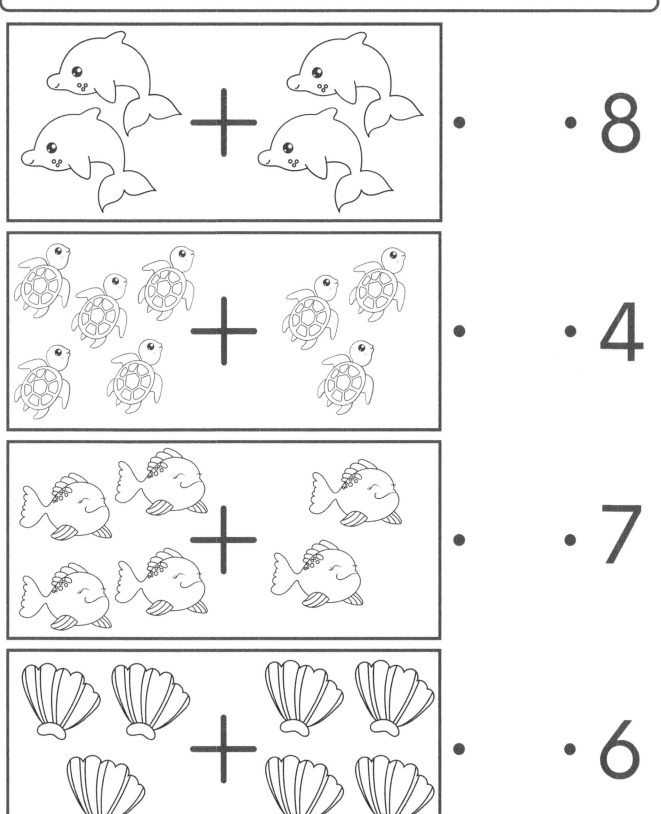

Subtraction

Find the missing number to solve each subtraction equation.

$$9 - \underline{} = 6$$

$$4 - \underline{} = 4$$

$$8 - \underline{} = 1$$

$$6 - \underline{} = 3$$

Subtraction

There are 9 muffins on the tray

Bobby ate 4 muffins

How many muffins are left?

$$\boxed{} - \boxed{} = \boxed{}$$

There are 7 fishes in a pond

5 fishes swim away

How many fishes are left in the pond?

$$\boxed{} - \boxed{} = \boxed{}$$

Dice Addition

Add the numbers together to find the total.

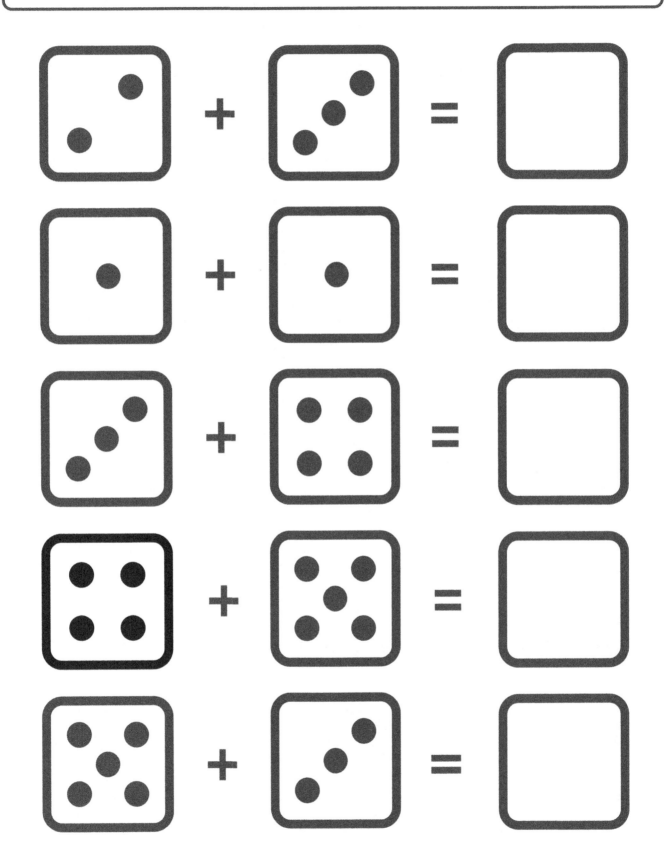

Addition

Susan saw 4 crabs

Nick saw 5 crabs

How many crabs did they see all together?

$$\boxed{} + \boxed{} = \boxed{}$$

Matthew had 4 balls

Monica gave him 2 more

How many balls does Benny have in all?

$$\boxed{} + \boxed{} = \boxed{}$$

Add or Subtract?

Write the correct symbol in each problem
(– or +)

$$7 - 5 = 2$$

$$4 \quad 3 = 7$$

$$5 \quad 1 = 6$$

$$8 \quad 4 = 4$$

Add or Subtract?

Write the correct symbol in each problem
(– or +)

$9 \quad 1 = 10$

$7 \quad 6 = 1$

$2 \quad 2 = 0$

$3 \quad 6 = 9$

Dice Addition

Add the numbers together to find the total.

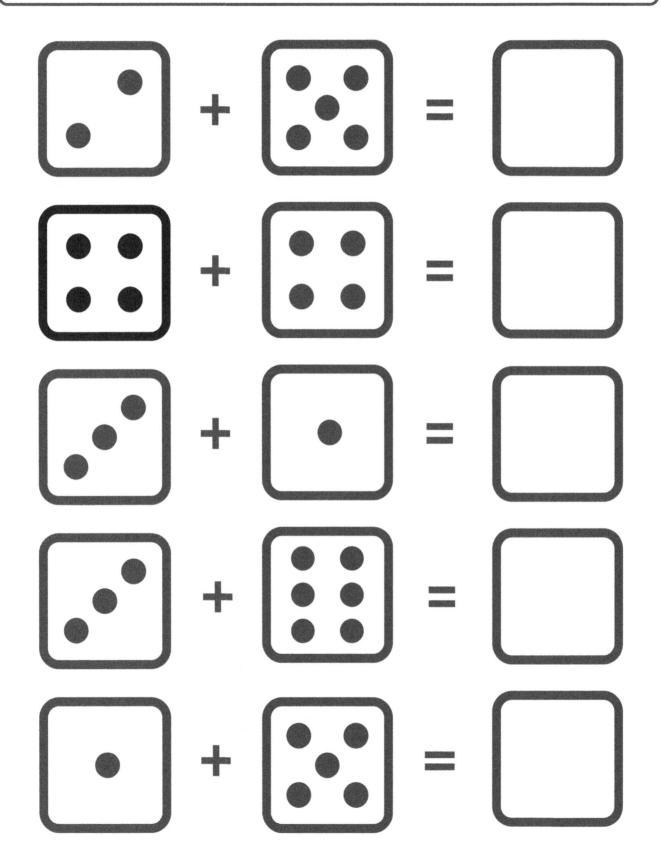

Addition

There are 5 eggs in a basket

3 more are added

How many eggs are there now?

$$\boxed{} + \boxed{} = \boxed{}$$

Lora has 4 red pens

2 yellow pens and 3 blue pens

How many pens does she have in all?

$$\boxed{} + \boxed{} + \boxed{} = \boxed{}$$

Number Bonds

Fill in the missing number in each number bond.

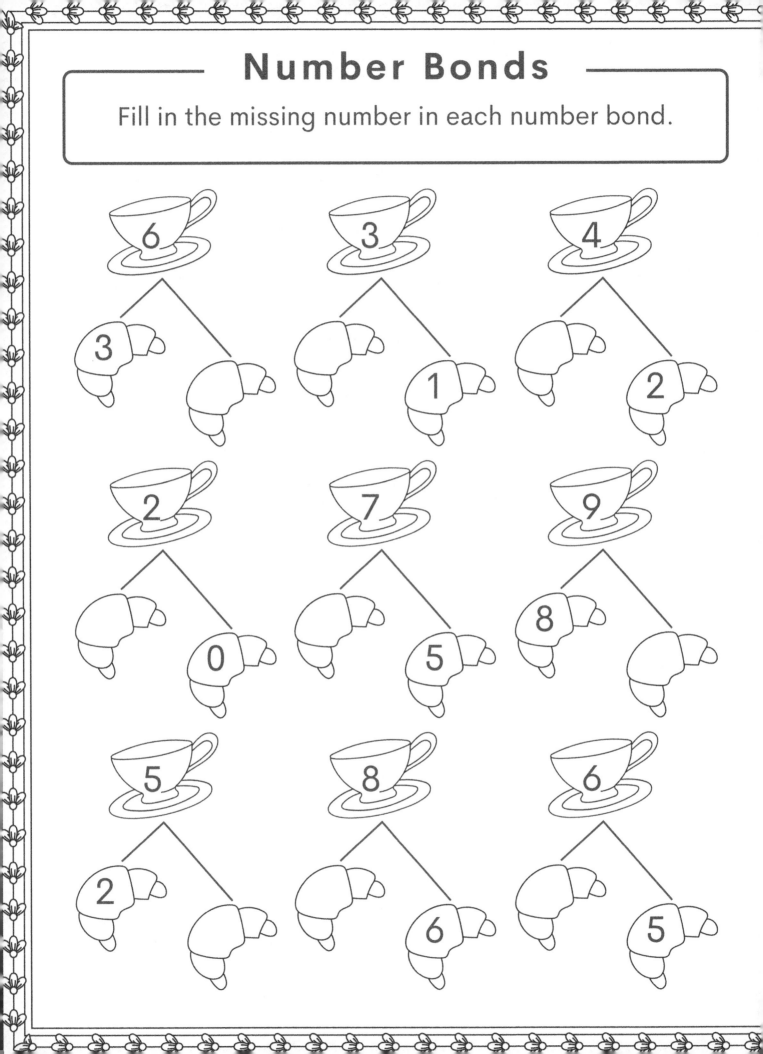

Subtraction

The dog has 6 bones

he eats 4 bones

How many bones are left?

☐ − ☐ = ☐

There are 7 birds in the tree

5 birds flew away

How many birds are left in the tree?

☐ − ☐ = ☐

Addition

Complete the circles with the right numbers,
so that the result of the addition is 10.

$\bigcirc$
$+$
6
$=$
$4 + \bigcirc =$ 10 $= \bigcirc + 9$
$=$ $=$
8 3
$\bigcirc +$ $+ \bigcirc$

Number Bonds

Fill in the missing number in each number bond.

Make 10

Fill in the blank boxes to make 10.

$7 + \boxed{} = \boxed{10}$

$\boxed{} + 4 = \boxed{10}$

$5 + \boxed{} = \boxed{10}$

$\boxed{} + 2 = \boxed{10}$

$9 + \boxed{} = \boxed{10}$

Subtraction

Peter has 7 flowers

He gives Sara 5 flowers

How many flowers does Peter have left?

□ − □ = □

Lora had 5 donuts

She ate 2 of them

How many donuts does Lora have left?

□ − □ = □

Write the missing number

| | 12 | 13 | 14 | 15 | 16 | 17 | 18 | 19 | 20 |

11   eleven

Trace and Write the Number 11

11 11 11 11 11 11

11

eleven eleven

Write the missing number

| 11 | ☐ | 13 | 14 | 15 | 16 | 17 | 18 | 19 | 20 |

12   twelve

Trace and Write the Number 12

12 12 12 12 12 12

12

twelve twelve

Write the missing number

11 12 □ 14 15 16 17 18 19 20

13 thirteen

Trace and Write the Number 13

13 13 13 13 13

13

thirteen

Write the missing number

11 12 13 □ 15 16 17 18 19 20

14 fourteen

Trace and Write the Number 14

14 14 14 14 14 14

14

fourteen

Write the missing number

| 11 | 12 | 13 | 14 | ☐ | 16 | 17 | 18 | 19 | 20 |

15   fifteen

Trace and Write the Number 15

15 15 15 15 15

15

fifteen

Write the missing number

| 11 | 12 | 13 | 14 | 15 | ☐ | 17 | 18 | 19 | 20 |

16   sixteen

Trace and Write the Number 16

16   16   16   16   16

16

sixteen

Write the missing number

| 11 | 12 | 13 | 14 | 15 | 16 | ☐ | 18 | 19 | 20 |

17 seventeen

Trace and Write the Number 17

17 17 17 17 17

17

seventeen

Write the missing number

11 12 13 14 15 16 17 ☐ 19 20

18   eighteen

Trace and Write the Number 18

18 18 18 18 18

18

eighteen

Write the missing number

11 12 13 14 15 16 17 18 ☐ 20

19   nineteen

Trace and Write the Number 19

19 19 19 19 19 19 19 19

19

nineteen

Write the missing number

| 11 | 12 | 13 | 14 | 15 | 16 | 17 | 18 | 19 | ☐ |

20 twenty

Trace and Write the Number 20

20 20 20 20 20

20

twenty

Match the numbers

Draw a line to match the number to its name.

16 •   • thirteen

11 •   • seventeen

19 •   • eleven

14 •   • sixteen

13 •   • fourteen

17 •   • nineteen

12 •   • twelve

15 •   • fifteen

18 •   • twenty

20 •   • eighteen

Skip Counting

Skip count by 5 and write the missing numbers to help the princess find the right way to the castle.

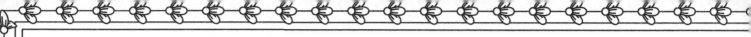

Before and After

Write the numbers that come before and after.

14   **15**   16

17

19

11

12

Before and After

Write the numbers that come before and after.

_____ 18 _____

_____ 10 _____

_____ 13 _____

_____ 16 _____

_____ 14 _____

Complete the Puzzle

Determine what each of the images represents in the following maths problems.

Find And Count

Count how many of each object you see and
write the correct number in each box.

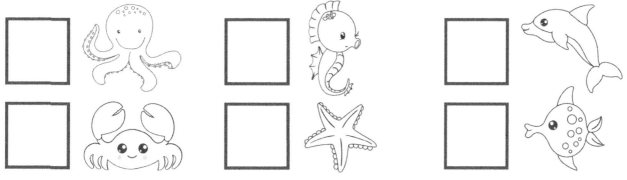

Before

Write the number that comes before these numbers.

11 12 13

___ 14 15

___ 17 18

___ 19 20

___ 16 17

Before

Write the number that comes before these numbers.

--------------- 10 11---------------

--------------- 18 19---------------

--------------- 11 12---------------

--------------- 13 14---------------

--------------- 15 16---------------

Complete the Puzzle

Determine what each of the images
represents in the following maths problems.

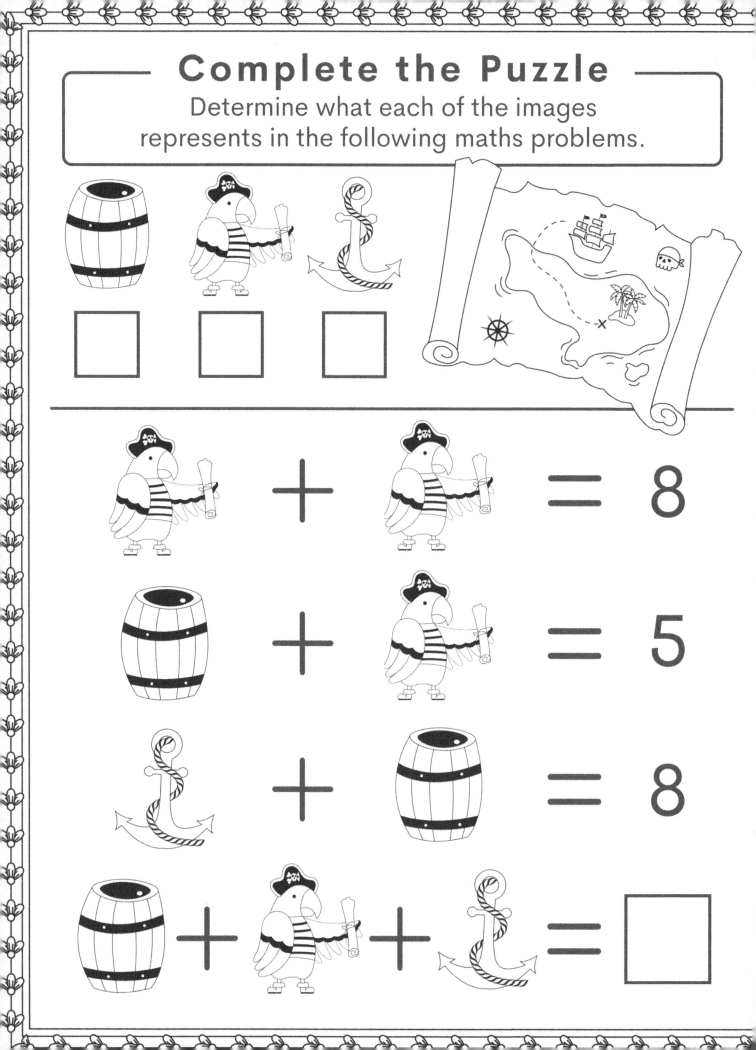

Find And Count

Count how many of each object you see and write the correct number in each box.

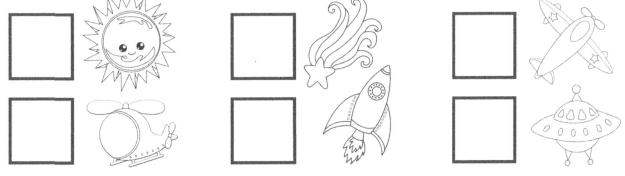

After

Write the number that comes after these numbers.

10 11 12

15 16 ____

18 19 ____

11 12 ____

14 15 ____

After

Write the number that comes after these numbers.

12 13

16 17

13 14

17 18

9 10

Skip Counting

Skip count by 5 and write the missing numbers.

Complete the Puzzle

Determine what each of the images represents in the following maths problems.

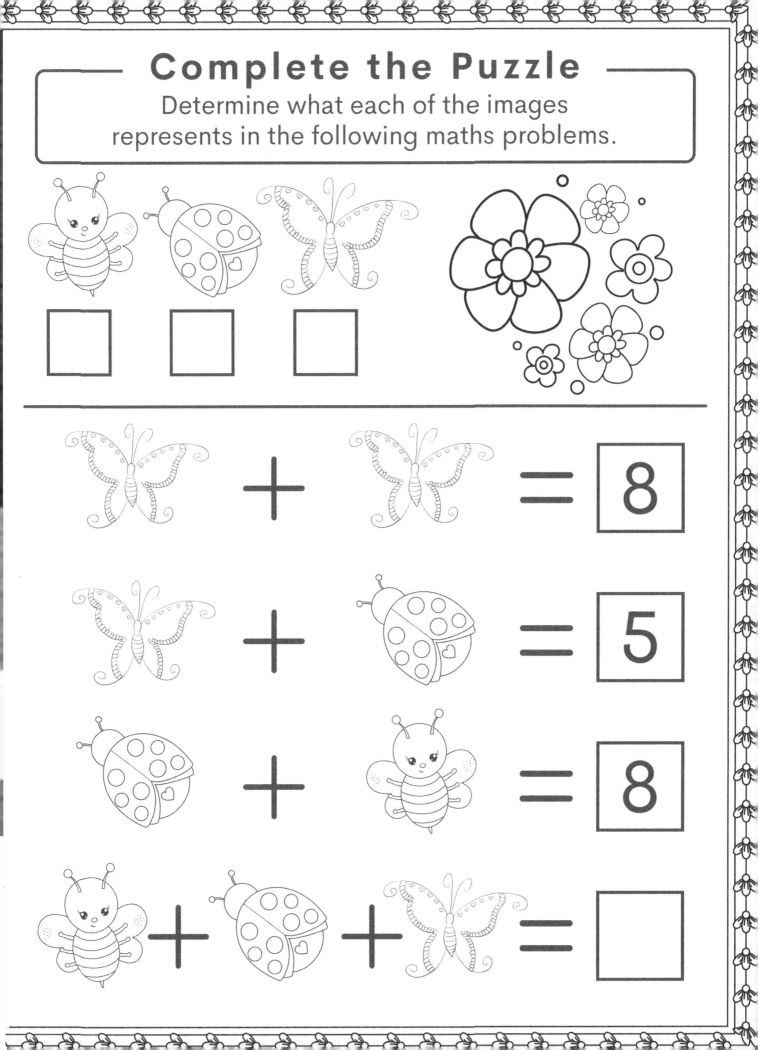

☐ ☐ ☐

🦋 + 🦋 = **8**

🦋 + 🐞 = **5**

🐞 + 🐝 = **8**

🐝 + 🐞 + 🦋 = ☐

Between

Write the number that comes between these numbers.

12   13   14

17   19

10   12

14   16

15   17

Between

Write the number that comes between these numbers.

18 _ _ _ _ _ _ _ _ _ 20

11 _ _ _ _ _ _ _ _ _ 13

16 _ _ _ _ _ _ _ _ _ 18

13 _ _ _ _ _ _ _ _ _ 15

9 _ _ _ _ _ _ _ _ _ 11

Complete the Puzzle

Determine what each of the images represents in the following maths problems.

$$\text{(mermaid)} + \text{(mermaid)} = 4$$

$$\text{(wheel)} + \text{(mermaid)} = 8$$

$$\text{(dolphin)} + \text{(wheel)} = 14$$

$$\text{(wheel)} + \text{(mermaid)} + \text{(dolphin)} = \boxed{}$$

Find And Count

Count how many of each object you see and
write the correct number in each box.

Before, Between, And After!

Write the numbers that come before, between, and after.

before	between	after
— 12	15 — 17	11 —
— 17	12 — 14	15 —
— 13	17 — 19	18 —
— 16	11 — 13	14 —
— 19	16 — 18	13 —

Skip Counting

Skip count by 5 and write the missing numbers.

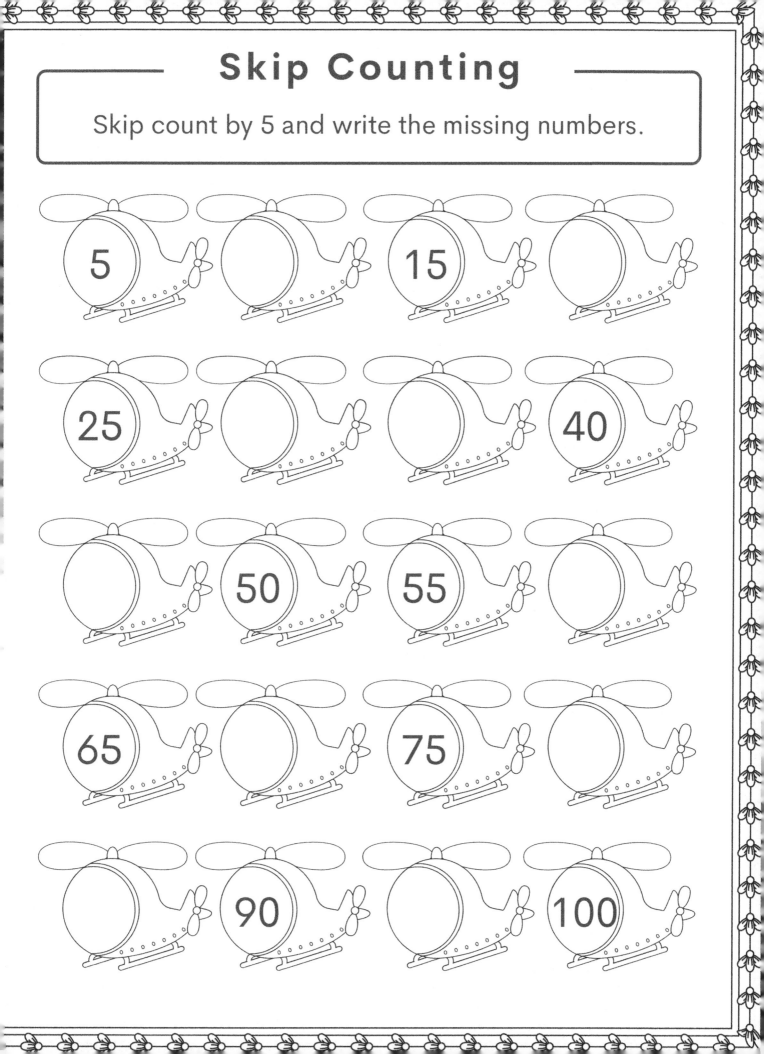

5   15

25   40

50 55

65   75

90   100

Greater Than, Less Than, Equal to

Write in each circle with the correct symbol.

> is greater than	= is equal to	< is less than
14 > 12	13 = 13	11 < 15
4 is greater than 2	3 is equal to 3	1 is less than 5

13 ◯ 19   11 ◯ 20

18 ◯ 10   18 ◯ 13

14 ◯ 11   12 ◯ 12

15 ◯ 15   16 ◯ 14

Greater Than, Less Than, Equal to

Write in each circle with the correct symbol.

15 ◯ 16   20 ◯ 20

17 ◯ 17   17 ◯ 15

12 ◯ 19   16 ◯ 19

18 ◯ 10   11 ◯ 11

16 ◯ 12   10 ◯ 13

20 ◯ 11   14 ◯ 15

Find And Count

Count how many of each object you see and
write the correct number in each box.

Comparing Number

Compare the numbers by using the right symbol.

> is greater than   = is equal to   < is less than

11 ☐ 19	3 ☐ 11	6 ☐ 7
2 ☐ 2	7 ☐ 13	17 ☐ 3
9 ☐ 5	12 ☐ 12	10 ☐ 20
8 ☐ 1	6 ☐ 5	4 ☐ 14
16 ☐ 18	3 ☐ 1	15 ☐ 15

Skip Counting

Skip count by 10 and write the missing numbers to help the bus find the right way to the school.

Count to 100

Fill in the missing numbers and count to 100.

1	2		4	5	6		8	9	10
11	12		14	15	16	17	18		20
21	22	23	24		26		28	29	
		33		35	36		38		40
41	42		44		46		48	49	
51		53		55		57	58		60
	62		64		66	67	68	69	70
71		73	74	75		77	78		80
81	82	83	84		86		88	89	90
	92	93		95	96	97		99	100

Made in United States
North Haven, CT
19 December 2022

29634880R00065